MONEY MAYHEM

The Bewildering Consequences of Cutting Money Free

JOHN LOOBY

Published by Oak Tree Press, Cork, Ireland

www.oaktreepress.com / www.SuccessStore.com

© 2018 John Looby

A catalogue record of this book is available from the British Library.

ISBN 978 1 78119 356 3 (paperback)

ISBN 978 1 78119 357 0 (ePub)

ISBN 978 1 78119 358 7 (Kindle)

ISBN 978 1 78119 359 4 (PDF)

Cover design: Kieran O'Connor

Cover image: iStock / gyener

CONTENTS

DEDICATION

To the *Yamamori* lunch crew – you know who you are – and to many more years of grappling joyously with the unanswerable.

John Looby
July 2018

INTRODUCTION

The world changed on 15 August 1971. After almost a quarter of a millennium broadly tied to gold, the money of the world was cut free. The consequences have been dramatic and far-reaching. And we are still grappling with them.

The pressured decision of an ultimately disgraced US President a mere generation ago to break with centuries of accepted wisdom changed our world – and continues to profoundly affect our lives.

Developments as disparate and apparently unrelated as the outcome of the Cold War, the accelerating pattern of *boom, bubble & bust*, and the stunning rise of China stem directly from that historic, and historically recent, decision.

Since that seminal night in the White House, we are all hostage to a compellingly incentivised and bewilderingly diverse money creation machine. Moreover, the political and monetary authorities in whom we trust are little more than impotent accommodators of an unmoored monetary mayhem beyond their control; a mayhem, in truth, beyond *any* control.

PROLOGUE

The fall of Rome in 476 AD is one of the most significant and widely debated events in history. For many, the progressive collapse of the monetary economy played a pivotal role in the descent of much of Europe into the Dark Ages.

The purity and weight – in other words, the intrinsic value – of the silver denarius had been sacrosanct to Romans for centuries. As a unit of account, a means of exchange and a store of value, it played a key role in the monetary stability and economic success of the greatest Empire the world had ever known.

This began to change in 64 AD, following the great fire that destroyed much of the eternal city. Rather than raise taxes to fund the massive re-building work, the pressured Emperor Nero chose to scale back the purity and weight of the silver denarius. The long journey towards monetary collapse had begun.

By the late 3rd century, the silver denarius had been debased to the point that it contained just 0.02% of silver, and confidence in its value had all but evaporated. The economic destruction wrought on the middle class and their savings had brought the Empire to the brink of civil breakdown. The attempt by the Emperor Diocletian to stabilise the economy by rebasing the denarius to close to its intrinsic value proved a jolting failure, as the lack of silver caused trade and activity to contract sharply.

Falling tax revenues eventually forced direct state appropriation of cattle and food and the consequent abandonment of land. This progressive collapse of the monetary economy helped fracture the weakening Empire, before it finally succumbed to the Barbarian onslaught.

The collapse of classical civilisation into the often-chaotic world of the Middle Ages unleashed enormous political, economic and social change. However, the challenge of successfully grappling with issues of money and value remained just as pressing as in the days of Diocletian.

A brief glance at monetary history confirms the regularity of dramatic upheaval. Periods of gold or other intrinsic standards have gyrated or co-existed with periods of private credit or sovereign money systems. Ultimately, the power of the sovereign to decide what it will accept in settlement of tax and other liabilities has been decisive in determining what can function as *money*.

One of the more unusual and long-lasting examples of this was the tally stick. Popular throughout medieval Europe, the tally stick became a sovereign money system in England under King Henry I and tally sticks were still circulating in parts of the Kingdom until the early 19th century.

The split tally was a stick marked with a system of notches and then split lengthwise with one half spent into the community by the King and the other half retained by his exchequer. Accepted as payment of taxes by the

Crown and consequently accepted as a means of exchange throughout the realm, the regime as it operated in the England of the late 12th century is described by Richard Fitz-Neal:

> *The manner of cutting is as follows. At the top of the tally a cut is made, the thickness of the palm of the hand, to represent a thousand pounds; then a hundred pounds by a cut the breadth of a thumb; twenty pounds, the breadth of a little finger; a single pound, the width of a swollen barleycorn; a shilling rather narrower; then a penny is marked by a single cut without removing any wood.*

It is important to remember that the quaint-sounding tally stick is not just a curiosity from the pre-modern period, but has often been a forerunner of more modern and brutal expressions of sovereign power in monetary matters.

The Hut Tax, and the central role it played in the expansion of the British Empire in Africa and elsewhere in the 19th and early 20th centuries, is a particularly infamous example. To the pain of many, the monetary insights of Henry I had been well-learned and were ruthlessly implemented by his successors and their minions.

The long centuries from warring feudal fiefdoms to modern sovereign states saw Europe and the wider world transformed. The regular waging of war in this process of jagged change saw the growing need for an internationally accepted unit of account. The tally sticks and their sovereign-determined cousins would not suffice as a means of exchange acceptable to increasingly in-demand mercenary soldiers, or as a unit of account recognised beyond the borders of any feudal warlord, however powerful.

GOLD

Fundamentally, the often-violent rivalries and regularly shifting alliances across Europe, and then the globe, from the late 16th to the mid-20th century were a desperate and relentless struggle to secure, control and accumulate the increasingly accepted global unit of account, means of exchange and store of value: gold.

In the bloody scramble for mastery of this vital cog of sovereign power, Cortes, Pizarro and their fellow *conquistadors* enslaved a new world, while in desperate response, the Albion *privateers* Raleigh, Drake and their successors harassed, and ultimately eclipsed, their bitter Iberian rivals.

Among much else, this ultimate ascent of Britannia was captured colourfully by Keynes in his insightful 1930 essay, *Economic Possibilities for our Grandchildren:*

> *For I trace the beginnings of British foreign investment to the treasure which Drake stole from Spain in 1580. In that year, he returned to England bringing with him the prodigious spoils of the Golden Hind. Queen Elizabeth was a considerable shareholder in the syndicate which had financed the expedition. Out of her share she paid off the whole of England's foreign debt, balanced her Budget, and*

found herself with about £40,000 in hand. This she invested in the Levant Company – which prospered. Out of the profits of the Levant Company, the East India Company was founded; and the profits of this great enterprise were the foundation of England's subsequent foreign investment. Now it happens that £40,000 accumulating at 3½ per cent compound interest approximately corresponds to the actual volume of England's foreign investments at various dates, and would amount to-day to the total of £4,000,000,000 which I have already quoted as being what our foreign investments now are. Thus, every £1 which Drake brought home in 1580 has now become £100,000.

For the great powers in the four centuries following the lucrative escapades of Raleigh and Drake, the frenzied imperial expansions and increasingly devastating wars were both fuelled by, and a relentless pursuit of, the glinting yellow *grail* underpinning sovereign power.

The gold standard was the effective global monetary regime from well before its formal adoption by Great Britain in 1717 to *the shutting of the gold window* by US President Richard Nixon in 1971. While its operation was sometimes suspended, or tweaked, in response to war, revolution or depression, the general adherence of most of the globe to this fixed intrinsic standard was a largely unquestioned constant in political, economic and social life.

The reason for this adherence was the widespread conviction summarised memorably again by Keynes - this time in his 1919 book, *The Economic Consequences of the Peace:*

> *Lenin was right. There is no subtler, no surer means of overturning the existing basis of society than to debauch the currency. The process engages all the hidden forces of economic law on the side of destruction, and does it in a manner which not one man in a million can diagnose.*

To avoid such a sinister calamity, few questioned the basic rationale of the gold standard, and the seemingly obvious observation of the legendary financier JP Morgan in 1893:

> *Gold is money. Everything else is credit.*

BRETTON WOODS

In more recent times, the monetary structure of the post-war world constructed at the famous Bretton Woods conference in July 1944 clearly adhered to this age-old belief. The soon-to-be-victorious allies, with the United States now the dominant leader, were determined to build a credible and durable monetary structure to promote post-war trade and recovery.

The cornerstone of this structure was that the 44 countries at Bretton Woods agreed to peg their currencies to the US dollar, which in turn was pegged to gold at a rate of $35 per ounce. In effect, the monetary structure of the world was now anchored to the dollar, which in turn was anchored to gold.

In the wake of Allied victory, the United States dominated the global economy. The Soviet Union may have been a credible military and geopolitical rival in 1945, but there was only one economic superpower. With much of Europe and Asia in physical and financial ruin, the US was the *de facto* industrial engine and credit provider to a devastated world.

In contrast to their predecessors at the end of the Great War, US policymakers firmly grasped this historic power and responsibility. Consciously rejecting the myopic mistakes of Versailles and its aftermath, they resisted, and then reversed, the instinctive dash to the comfort of isolation.

Significantly, this rejection of isolationism, and the clear-eyed determination to embrace and shape the post-war world, became a shared goal across the domestic political divide.

Championing the United Nations, the Marshall Plan and then NATO, Democrat President Truman greatly burnished the open vision of his iconic predecessor. On the other side of the aisle, Eisenhower abandoned fêted retirement to serve as the first Secretary General of NATO, defeat isolationist rival Robert Taft for the Republican Presidential nomination in 1952, and then convincingly win the White House.

Unsurprisingly keen to exploit their power in shaping the post-war global monetary system – most crucially by insisting that the dollar emerged from Bretton Woods as the global reserve currency – US policymakers also displayed a deft understanding of the shared benefits of better times for both friend and former foe alike.

Much to the chagrin of Keynes, the critical outcome of Bretton Woods was that the world needed dollars. In practical terms, this meant that, until the world could sell its goods and services to US buyers to receive dollars in exchange, or regain its credit-worthiness with US banks to borrow them, the enlightened self-interest of US policy was content to all but give them away.

Marshall Aid, broad support for the nascent European Coal & Steel Community, and the preferential trade access afforded to Japan and others, were just some of the policies designed to supply much-needed dollars to a desperate world.

Against this backdrop of monetary stability and enlightened US self-interest, post-war global trade expanded rapidly helping to fuel a remarkable and sustained global recovery. Fondly remembered by many, the post-war decades up to the early 1970s were a golden era of social and economic progress across much of the *free* world.

While the Cold War challenge of the Soviet Union was likely to be lengthy, costly and uncertain, the position of the US as the dominant global producer and creditor seemed secure. Indeed, as the prosperous contentment of the Eisenhower era gave way to the youthful promise of Kennedy and the *New Frontier*, the stability and success of the US-led West – anchored monetarily *via* the dollar on gold – seemed solidly and confidently assured.

The chink in this structure proved to be the implicit necessity for the anchor country, the United States, to manage its economy so that its peg to gold remained credible. Those who held dollars needed to believe that their dollars would always be convertible into gold, the anchor store of value.

Dragged ever deeper into the costly folly of the Vietnam War, with a growing balance of payments deficit and a quickening flow of dollars to the rest of the world, President Richard Nixon fatally undermined the credibility of the dollar link to gold. While the impossible dreams of his predecessor – to build a *Great Society* at home, while fighting an increasingly expensive and futile war in South East Asia – certainly contributed, the fateful decision to effectively cut money free was ultimately made by Nixon.

By the early autumn of 1971, the persistent appearance of France and other creditors at the *gold window* in Washington, seeking to convert their growing stock of dollars into gold, left Nixon facing an unenviable choice on that hot August night a mere generation ago. He could continue to convert the dollars presented into gold and thereby exhaust the gold reserves of the United States, or refuse to do so, and smash the cornerstone of the global monetary structure.

Nixon chose the latter. As a result, having effectively been a constant in human affairs for over a quarter of a millennium, the gold standard formalised by Newton in London in 1717 and subsequently adopted around the globe, was ended by Presidential *fiat* in Washington.

A new global monetary order – a changed world with bewildering consequences – had dawned.

THE DOLLAR

The United States is now in the unprecedented position of being the issuer of an *unanchored* global reserve currency. By contrast, and however reluctantly, the rest of the world is now in the unenviable position of being the forced user of the unmoored US dollar.

As tellingly underlined by Nixon Treasury Secretary John Connally to his G-10 counterparts in November 1971:

> *The dollar is our currency, but your problem.*

Remarkably, the break with gold has served to strengthen – rather than weaken – the dominance of the dollar. In effect, since the end of Bretton Woods, the gold standard has given way to the dollar standard.

Crucially, the hegemonic position of the dollar was cemented by the decision of the major oil exporting countries – led by Saudi Arabia – to exclusively demand dollars in payment for their precious output.

While the background to this decision is clouded in the opaque world of geopolitical manoeuvring and shuttle diplomacy, the practical and critical outcome is that the world still needs dollars. Regardless of the diplomatic and other machinations involved, the US ensured that the demise of the gold anchor was followed, all but seamlessly, by the birth of the petrodollar. If Sweden, for example, wants to buy oil from its Nordic neighbour Norway, it must buy or borrow dollars to execute the transaction. The same is true for oil importers everywhere.

Underpinned by the birth of the petrodollar, the dominance of the dollar accrues significant benefits to the US. The ever more aptly named *exorbitant privilege* – the phrase coined by French Finance Minister Giscard d'Estaing in the 1960s as the pressure on Bretton Woods mounted – enables the US to effectively exchange costless promises for valuable goods, services and assets, thereby enabling US citizens to consistently consume more than they produce.

This excess consumption – the balance of payments current account deficit – has averaged around 3% of GDP annually, and has now been a consistent feature of the US and global economy for decades.

Although the US economy today is roughly the same size as the EU – accounting for just over one-fifth of global GDP – the dollar still accounts for almost three-quarters of global foreign exchange reserves, and almost nine-tenths of global foreign exchange transactions.

Clearly, the world still needs – and therefore demands – dollars. Notwithstanding the relative decline of the US economy, the dollar remains the QWERTY keyboard of the global monetary system.

THE COLD WAR

Ironically, the Nixon Administration failed to appreciate the extraordinary power conferred on it by the decision to unmoor the dollar from gold. Despite Connally's intuition, they failed to make the connection between this historic decision and the new dynamic it injected into the historic Cold War struggle with the Soviet Union.

The 1970s was a difficult decade for the United States. From wearying stagflation to the humiliation of Saigon, and the shame of Watergate to the surge of the Sandinistas, it was a time plagued by a pervasive sense of national decline.

The debacle of *Operation Eagle Claw* in April 1980 was particularly painful and seemed to summarise acutely the growing impotence of a great power in inevitable retreat. The bloody failure to rescue US hostages in Tehran seemed stark confirmation of an ongoing loss of influence amid a prolonged Cold War stalemate. Captive hostages at the embassy and dead would-be rescuers on enemy sand were depressing symbols of loss and foreboding. Warily managing the messy process of descent seemed to be the inescapable reality for occupants of the Oval Office.

Into this troubled time, a smiling ex-B-movie star was elected President in November 1980. Facing the implacable foe of the Soviet Union and the apparently rigid constraints of yawning twin deficits, his mantra that it was now *Morning in America* seemed naïvely optimistic.

Most especially, his stubborn refusal to follow the prevailing policy of containing the threat from the Eastern bloc seemed hopelessly at odds with the long-term reality of effective superpower balance.

Indeed, five years into his Presidency, in an article to mark the 40th anniversary of the Cold War division of Europe, and undoubtedly reflecting the conventional wisdom of the time, *The Economist* magazine confidently concluded that the prospects for change were all but non-existent:

Nothing much will have changed by 2025.

And yet we now know that, within six weeks of publication of this article, the steady march to rapid Cold War victory was well underway. The smiling President Reagan faced the fragile Secretary General Gorbachev in Reykjavik to effectively begin the process of managing the orderly collapse of Soviet power.

For Reagan, the unmooring of the dollar by Nixon ultimately paved the way for the US to spend the Soviet Union into submission – and, ultimately, destruction.

As the issuer of the global reserve currency, Reagan faced no constraint in rapidly accelerating military spending and simultaneously slashing taxes, while his Cold War adversary soon buckled under the pressure to keep up.

Remarkably, the impossibly delusional goal of a seemingly naïve President came to pass.

More remarkably still, the fundamental cause of Cold War victory was not the determined optimism of the popular Reagan, but the unexpected consequence of the pressured decision of his generally despised rival to cut money free.

THE GEITHNER
DOCTRINE

Freed of the Bretton Woods anchor, the major central banks such as the US Federal Reserve, the Bank of England, the Bank of Japan and the ECB can create unlimited quantities of domestic money. They simply credit the accounts of their member institutions with a keystroke – in dollars, sterling, yen or euro respectively – as and when required.

The extent of this new freedom was most clearly displayed in the aftermath of the collapse of Lehman Brothers in September 2008, and the dramatic intensification of the *global financial crisis*.

The decision by Bush Treasury Secretary Hank Paulson to effectively allow the bankruptcy of a medium-sized US investment bank – Lehman Brothers – sparked a massive contraction in global credit, trade and activity. The lesson was not lost on his young successor, Obama Treasury Secretary, Timothy Geithner.

There are numerous reasons why historians like to characterise significant policy positions as *doctrines*. Usually, the elevation of a policy to the status of a doctrine is a signal of a change with major implications for the future.

For example:

- o The *Monroe doctrine* of 1823 saw newly re-elected US President Monroe warn that "further efforts by European nations to colonise land or interfere with states in North or South America would be viewed as acts of aggression". The end of European interference in the Western Hemisphere is directly traceable to this doctrine.

- o Over a century later, the *Truman doctrine* of 1947 – justifying US involvement in the Greek civil war – set the scene for East / West confrontation around the globe for much of the next half-century.

- o More recently, the *Bush doctrine* following 9/11/2001 – asserting the right of the US to wage preventive war in self-defence – signalled over a decade and a half (and counting) of US military engagement in Afghanistan, Iraq and elsewhere.

The Geithner doctrine has never been formally stated in public. However, a policy of protecting bank depositors and their legal equivalents – regardless of the losses of their banks – has been unbreakably in place since his period in office. Moreover, this doctrine has been adopted as an all but universal tenet around the globe.

Buttressed by the Geithner doctrine, monetary policymakers – confronting the greatest financial crisis since 1929 and undeniably shocked by the precipitous post-Lehman collapse in global trade and activity – aggressively deployed the freedom of unmoored money to effectively guarantee bank depositors and their legal equivalents across the developed world.

The simple, practical mechanics of this extraordinary freedom and promise was summarised at the time by then US Federal Reserve Chairman Ben Bernanke, in reply to a question from Scott Pelley on the US TV show *60 Minutes*:

> *Pelley asked: "Is that tax money that the Fed is spending?"*
>
> *Bernanke replied: "It's not tax money. The banks have accounts with the Fed, much the same way that you have an account in a commercial bank. So, to lend to a bank, we simply use the computer to mark up the size of the account that they have with the Fed".*

Crucially, this promise by the Fed to US banks became an effective promise to major banks across the globe. Prompted by the growing risk of non-US banks facing a run from their dollar creditors, the six major central banks – the Fed, the ECB, the BOJ, the BOE, the SNB, and the BOC – concluded a currency swap deal, which in practice saw the Fed make dollar loans to the other central banks as and when needed. In the trauma of the crisis, this deal ensured that all six were now a credible *lender of last resort* to their respective banks, who in turn were now credible counterparties to their creditors.

Strikingly, while the currency swap deal was initially envisaged as a temporary arrangement to overcome the emergency of the crisis, it became permanent in October

2013. In practice, it renders the Geithner doctrine impregnable.

Free to reject the risk of another Lehman, the message that bank creditors in dollars, euro, yen, sterling, Swiss francs, and Canadian dollars will necessarily be made whole in full and on time by the relevant Central Bank has been made clear and has been broadly understood.

The Geithner doctrine underpinned the pay-outs by the Irish government to depositors and their legal equivalents in failed banks in Ireland. It also underpinned the UK government pay-outs to British depositors and their legal equivalents in failed British and Icelandic banks. As recently as the summer of 2017, the Italian government similarly made whole the equivalent liabilities of two failed banks in Italy.

The consequent collapse in global bond yields and credit spreads – regardless of the individual travails of the underlying debtor – has strongly underlined this message in the period since.

More particularly, the broad understanding in financial markets that depositors and their legal equivalents in banks across the developed world are now effectively guaranteed by the relevant Central Bank, and ultimately the relevant government, is all but beyond debate.

The recent case of Deutsche Bank is a good example of this general understanding, and of how the Geithner doctrine now stands without challenge.

DEUTSCHE BANK

The Prussian military victory over France in 1870 proved the decisive event in the forging of a new political and economic colossus.

At the heart of a humiliated France, in the famous Hall of Mirrors at the Palace of Versailles, Chancellor Otto von Bismarck of Prussia proclaimed a new unified German Empire in January 1871. The course of European, and indeed global history, was changed forever.

In parallel with its military success, the Prussian government was consciously seeking to extend its economic reach. Deutsche Bank was founded in Berlin in the same year as victory over France, with a government statute stating that:

> *The object of the company is to transact banking business to promote and facilitate trade relations between Germany, other European countries and overseas markets.*

Through the many upheavals of German history since, the central role and mission of Deutsche Bank has remained remarkably consistent.

The author and economist John Kay uses a striking analogy to describe much of the activity in banking and financial markets.

To shave journey time on a motorway, many drivers employ a *tailgating* strategy of driving very close to the car in front. Consequently, on almost all trips they succeed in arriving at their destination sooner, while very occasionally but often catastrophically they crash and cause a tragic pile-up.

In the aftermath of such a pile-up, there is always a proximate cause offered as an explanation – mechanical failure, driver error, tyre issues or whatever – while the real cause is the tailgating strategy, which will inevitably result in a pattern of many small gains followed by a dramatic and likely catastrophic loss. In addition to its broader relevance to much financial market activity, this insightful analogy speaks directly to the recent travails of Deutsche Bank.

The Deutsche Bank share price has fallen significantly in recent years. One notable phase of this fall was sparked at the end of September 2016 by a reported fine of $14bn imposed by the US Justice Department. However, the reported fine is best understood as just the latest bump in the road. The real cause of difficulty for Deutsche Bank, and its banking equivalents across the globe, is a balance sheet that means they are always travelling fast and very close to the vehicle in front.

Fundamentally, bank assets are generally supported by a relatively tiny sliver of equity, with the vast bulk funded by debt. Across the banking landscape of the developed world, the sliver of equity is leveraged around 23 times – a fall of just 4% in the value of bank assets would entirely wipe out shareholders. Moreover, there is a massive mismatch between the generally long-term maturity of bank assets, and the generally short-term maturity of bank debts.

Almost uniquely therefore, as was painfully highlighted in the period after the collapse of Lehman Brothers, banks are businesses that cannot survive without the backing of central banks and, ultimately, governments. If there was any doubt, for example, that the ECB and, ultimately, the German Government effectively stands behind the liabilities of Deutsche Bank, there would already have been a rush to the exits by bondholders and depositors. There has been no such rush.

Banks are different and are treated differently. In the absence of meaningful change, this is not a cyclical and temporary issue; it is structural and permanent. It is a universal and unchanging reality confirmed once again by the recent travails of Deutsche Bank. While the banks' vulnerabilities may be particularly acute, the interconnectedness of the system means that the chain is only as strong as the weakest link. The Geithner doctrine must be obeyed.

MONEY CUT FREE

In theory, cutting money free appears to confer great power on central banks. In practice, however, they are just the forced and automatic accommodators of the money creation decisions of the private banking, and broader financial, systems.

The Great Depression that followed the Wall Street crash of 1929 has been widely blamed on the flawed policy response of the US Federal Reserve. Most famously, the doyen of monetary economics, Milton Friedman, argued that the collapse of the US money supply by a third between 1929 and 1933 turned a brutal day on the stock market into a multi-year depression.

In Friedman's view, the failure of the Federal Reserve to maintain the money supply caused the vicious cycle of collapsing banks, activity and hope:

> *The Federal Reserve System could have prevented the decline (in the money supply) at all times. The terrible depression which followed the crash was a direct result of bungling by the Federal Reserve System.*

Ben Bernanke, the Fed Chairman during the global financial crisis, powerfully endorsed these views at Friedman's 90th birthday celebration in 2002:

> *Let me end my talk by abusing slightly my status as an official representative of the Federal Reserve. I would like to say to Milton and Anna: Regarding the Great Depression. You're right, we did it. We're very sorry. But thanks to you, we won't do it again.*

Central to the views of Friedman, Bernanke and the broader conventional wisdom is the assumed ability of the Federal Reserve, or any equivalent central bank, to broadly determine the money supply. In simple terms, as the controller of the effective dollar printing press, the Federal Reserve is assumed to be the exogenous controller of the quantity of money in the economy. In practice, the mechanism by which the Fed is assumed to exercise this control is familiar to all who have had the dubious pleasure of sitting through an economics class on the money multiplier.

As is invariably outlined for simplicity in such classes, assume that the reserve ratio set by the Fed for the banking system is 10% and that the Fed wants to increase the money supply by $1,000.

The Fed begins by effectively printing or keystroking $100 to buy $100 of US Treasury bonds on the open market. The seller of the bonds deposits her $100 proceeds at her bank, which puts $10 aside as the reserve and loans out $90 to a customer looking to pay his utility bill. The utility company deposits its $90 proceeds at its bank, which puts $9 aside as the reserve and loans out $81 to a customer looking to go to the opera. The opera company deposits its $81 proceeds at its bank and the process continues until a total of $1,000 in new money has been created – in other words, the policy objective of the Fed to increase the money supply by $1,000 has been achieved.

The fact that banks in the US, the UK and elsewhere no longer need to meet any reserve requirements has no relevance to this debate. The crucial point is the direction of causation. The Fed seemingly determines the money supply with the private banking system meekly accommodating its wishes. While Nixon may have smashed its age-old anchor, money nonetheless remains tethered to central bank control.

Unfortunately, for those comforted by belief in the wisdom and power of central banks, this conventional story of central bank control bears no relation to reality. Indeed, the reality of money creation is so at odds with the narrative of Friedman and Bernanke that it recalls the story of Irish writer Samuel Beckett when asked by a French journalist:

"Vous êtes Anglais, Monsieur Beckett?"

to which Beckett replied:

"Au contraire".

In practice, money creation runs in completely the opposite direction to the conventional view. Simply put, banks create money by granting loans, and crucially, this power is now effectively limitless. For example:

- A bank grants a loan of $10,000 to a customer to buy a car. The bank credits the current account of the customer, who writes a cheque for $10,000 to the seller of the car.

- The seller of the car deposits the cheque to her bank account. If this is the same bank as that of the car-buyer, this bank now has an asset in the form of the loan to the car-buyer, balanced by a liability in the form of the deposit from the car-seller.

- Alternatively, if the car-seller deposits the cheque at a different bank, the bank of the car-buyer will borrow $10,000 *via* the inter-bank market to transfer to the bank of the car-seller, and while having the same asset as before, it is now balanced in the form of this inter-bank loan.

The net effect of this process is that $10,000 has been created from nothing and is now circulating in the economy. The bank that granted the loan is profiting from charging a higher interest rate to its car-buying customer than it pays to either the car-selling depositor or, in the alternative case, to the inter-bank lender. This profit potential incentivises the bank to repeat the process as often and to the largest extent possible.

In theory, the conventionally-argued constraint on this is two-fold:

- o The bank must fulfil a *reserve ratio*.

- o The bank must also fulfil a *capital ratio*.

Fulfilling a reserve ratio requires the bank to hold a certain percentage of its assets in 'reserve' at the central bank. While, in theory, this enables the central bank to control the quantum of loans granted by the bank, in practice the central bank must acquiesce to the lending decisions of the bank by ensuring that sufficient reserves are always available for the bank to meet its reserve ratio. In practice, even in the era and in the countries where a reserve ratio exists, there is no reserve constraint on the bank loaning and thereby creating as much money as it chooses.

This reality was summarised clearly by economist Basil J. Moore in 1983:

> *Once deposits have been created by an act of lending, the central bank must ensure that the required reserves are available. Otherwise the banks, no matter how hard they scramble for funds, could not in aggregate meet their reserve requirements.*

Fulfilling a capital ratio requires the bank to hold a certain percentage of capital, such as equity provided by its shareholders, to its assets such as loans. While again, in theory, this enables the central bank to control the quantum of loans granted by the bank, in practice a bank determined to grant more loans is free both to increase its capital *via* retained profits and / or raise fresh capital without any interference from the central bank. In practice, there is little capital constraint on the bank loaning and thereby creating as much money as it chooses.

Arguably, the economist, author and diplomat John Kenneth Galbraith made the most memorable statement of this reality when wryly reflecting on the extraordinary power of private banks in his 1975 book, *Money: Whence It Came, Where It Went*:

> *The process by which banks create money is so simple that it repels the mind.*

Small wonder that money has exploded since Nixon cut it free. Banks, and subsequently shadow banks and the broader financial system, are overwhelmingly incentivised to do little else. For example, although unchanged for centuries, in less than four decades after the collapse of Bretton Woods bank assets in the UK as a % of GDP exploded by a factor greater than five.

The then Governor of the Bank of England, Sir Mervyn King, summarised this powerful dynamic at a speech in New York in 2010: *Banking – from Bagehot to Basel and Back Again*:

> *The size of the balance sheet (of banks) is no longer limited … banks (can) manufacture additional assets (loans) without limit … Gross (bank) balance sheets are not restricted …*

We live in a world where almost all our money is borrowed into existence. Created endogenously within the private banking and broader financial system, this money is borrowed by governments, households and corporations at interest rates higher than that paid on the liabilities created. Unsurprisingly, propelled by this compelling incentive and facing no effective constraint, the banking and broader financial system has unleashed an unprecedented money explosion.

THE MONEY
EXPLOSION

The pithy insight of US economist Hyman Minsky is particularly helpful in grappling with understanding this explosion:

> *Everyone can create money; the problem is to get it accepted.*

In practice, an unanchored global reserve currency, the Geithner doctrine and privately-created endogenous money have combined to overcome the problem. The unhindered capacity to create unlimited money – guaranteed by the major central banks, and therefore universally accepted – has unleashed an extraordinary money explosion.

In his 2015 book, *Other People's Money: The Real Business of Finance,* John Kay uses the more sobering term *financialisation* to capture this phenomenon. Opening with an evocative description of the towering skyscrapers of Wall Street and the City of London, he poses the seemingly simple question about the activities of their well-rewarded occupants:

> *But what do all these people do?*

With palpable bemusement, he then provides the answer:

> *To an extent that staggers the imagination, they deal with each other ... the assets of these banks mostly consist of claims on other banks. Their liabilities are mainly obligations to other financial institutions.*

While the detachment of the banking system from the *real* economy is remarkable, the behaviour of the broader financial system in exploiting its compelling incentive to create money is what really interests Kay:

> *The finance sector establishes claims against assets – the operating assets and future profits of a company, or the physical property and prospective earnings of an individual – and almost any such claim can be turned into a tradable security.*

One of the most well-known examples was probably the *Bowie Bond*. The wily singer raised $55m from investors in 1997, secured on the future revenues of the 25 albums he recorded before 1990. Even more significantly, as outlined again by Kay, the creation of such securities fuelled the further explosion of *derivatives*:

> *If securities are claims on assets, derivative securities are claims on other securities, and their value depends on the price, and ultimately on the value, of these underlying securities. Once you have created*

derivative securities, you can create further layers of
derivative securities whose values are dependent on
the values of other derivative securities – and so on.

For the most devoted followers of the legendary investor Warren Buffett, the biggest date in the diary is the annual general meeting of Berkshire Hathaway. Held every year in Buffett's hometown of Omaha, Nebraska, the so-called *Woodstock for Capitalists* has attracted over 30,000 shareholder fans in recent years.

Arguably of greater interest – certainly for those of us unlikely to make the pilgrimage to Omaha – is the release of the Berkshire Hathaway annual letter to shareholders. Since the first letter in 1965, Buffett has used this often-groundbreaking missive to share his thoughts on a wide range of issues. None have proven as prescient as his offering in 2002:

The range of derivatives contracts is limited only by
the imagination of man or sometimes, so it seems,
madmen ... The derivatives genie is now well out of
the bottle, and these instruments will almost certainly
multiply in variety and number until some event
makes their toxicity clear ... We view them as time
bombs, both for the parties that deal in them and the
economic system ... In our view, derivatives are
financial weapons of mass destruction, carrying
dangers that are potentially lethal ...

Ignoring Buffett, the explosion of *mortgage-backed securities* and related derivatives in the run-up to the global financial crisis warrants special mention.

With customary aplomb, the process was summarised by recent Nobel prize-winning economist Richard Thaler, and the actress Serena Gomez, in a memorable scene from the 2016 movie, *The Big Short*. Seated at a roulette table in a crowded casino, the unlikely duo explains the step-by-step explosion of the markets for mortgage-backed collateralised debt obligations (CDOs), synthetic CDOs, and credit default swaps (CDSs) – all securities or derivative securities ultimately dependent on a relatively small number of increasingly pressured US mortgage borrowers.

To the great shock of policymakers and investors across the globe, when some of these borrowers began to miss payments, the global financial system froze, and the greatest financial and economic upheaval since the great depression followed.

Since the fuse was lit by Nixon, unhampered financialisation has spawned an increasingly fragile economic system gingerly underpinned by a bewilderingly diverse array of densely interwoven, and dizzyingly opaque, promises. Crucially, these promises are ultimately backed not by those who make them, but by the major central banks and their necessarily passive governments. The explicit reality of this unstable asymmetry, where the default of debtors must not be allowed to impact the bulk of their creditors, is arguably the central, and enduring, legacy of the global financial crisis.

In short, we remain hostage to a banking and broader financial system compellingly incentivised and effectively unhindered from exploiting a stacked *heads I win / tails you lose* relationship with the rest of society. Contrary to much conventional economic thinking, the accelerating pattern of *boom, bubble & bust* should be little surprise.

BOOM, BUBBLE & BUST

Shortly after the collapse of Lehman Brothers in September 2008, Queen Elizabeth opened a new building at the London School of Economics. Amid the gathered dignitaries, including some world-renowned economists, she famously asked the question about the dramatic crisis dominating headlines across the world:

This is awful. Why did nobody see it coming?

In response, the British Academy convened a forum the following June of experts from business, the City, its regulators, academia and government, and summarised their answers in a letter to Buckingham Palace a month later. Tellingly, the letter is more a summary of the confusion that gripped conventional thinking than a satisfactory answer to the question. In truth, when the most serious financial and economic crisis since the great depression erupted, the response of conventional economic thinking can best be described as shock.

The period from the end of the Cold War until the global financial crisis had seemed to validate much conventional economic thought. More particularly, the march of globalisation, technology, financial innovation and free-market ideology had seemed to produce, and promise, a great moderation in the behaviour of the global economy.

For financial markets and policymakers, the tantalising prospect that, in the words of then UK Chancellor Gordon Brown:

We have eliminated boom and bust

seemed less a theoretical aspiration and more a self-evident success. When this proved delusional, the confession of long-time US Federal Reserve Chairman Alan Greenspan to a congressional committee in October 2008 memorably captured the new, shaken mood:

Yes, I've found a flaw (in my ideology). The modern risk management paradigm held sway for decades. The whole intellectual edifice, however, collapsed in the summer of last year and the crisis has turned out to be much broader than anything I could have imagined.

In a provocative speech in 2012, *The Dog & the Frisbee*, seeking to draw lessons for policymakers and regulators from the crisis, Andrew Haldane of the Bank of England neatly set the context for the enduring flaw in Greenspan's thinking:

Modern macroeconomics has its analytical roots in the general equilibrium framework of Kenneth Arrow and Gerard Debreu. In the Arrow-Debreu framework, the probability distribution of future states of the world is known by agents ... Modern finance has its origins in the portfolio allocation framework of Harry Markowitz and Robert Merton. This Merton-Markowitz framework assumes a known probability for future market risk ... Together, the Arrow-Debreu and Merton-Markowitz frameworks form the bedrock of modern macroeconomics and finance.

Unfortunately, we don't live in a world of the coin toss or the casino, where outcomes and their probabilities are known to us *ex ante*. We live in a world of wrenching uncertainty, where very often the most important outcomes are utterly unknowable. The trader, author and philosopher of uncertainty Nassim Taleb captures this memorably in his story of the turkey in the run-up to Thanksgiving:

A turkey is fed for 1,000 days – every day confirms to its statistical department that humans care about its welfare 'with increased statistical significance'. On the 1,001st day, the turkey has a surprise.

In parallel with the discrediting of the Arrow-Debreu and Merton-Markowitz frameworks, the *Financial Instability Hypothesis* of long-neglected US economist Hyman Minsky, first published in 1975, has been widely re-embraced. The characterisation by Minsky of the macro economy as a system prone to bouts of dramatic instability generated endogenously by the financial system chimed true with the experience before and after the collapse of Lehman Brothers. His key insight that stability can lead to instability plausibly captured the long post-Cold War stability and its shuddering denouement.

Financial crises, of course, have always been a feature of economic life. Certainly, since the advent of the modern market economy in the early 18th century, the pattern of vaulting boom followed by depressing bust has been a constant. While the details differ, there is little fundamental difference, for example, between the *South Sea bubble* that so entranced the London of Isaac Newton and the *property bubble* that so seduced the Ireland of Bertie Ahern. Unarguably, however, the post-Nixon world of endogenously-created explosive money is turbo-charging and accelerating this pattern.

According to the IMF, 147 individual banking crises have occurred between 1970 and 2011. Notwithstanding the relative economic stability between the fall of the Soviet Union and the collapse of Lehman Brothers, since Nixon cut money free the global financial system has been rocked successively by the *Latin-American Debt crisis,* the *Savings & Loans crisis,* the *Nikkei collapse,* the *Asian crisis,* the *Dot-Com collapse,* and the *global financial crisis.*

The Irish experience is illustrative and sobering. The *boom, bubble & bust* of the Irish property and banking collapse was generated by the borrowing and lending decisions of Irish borrowers and private Irish banks. Creating assets and liabilities from thin air in a recklessly accelerated hunt for illusionary profit, a near trebling in the outstanding stock of borrowing and lending by Irish banks in the six years to 2008 was the extraordinary, and ultimately devastating, outcome. More generally, the words of legendary investor Seth Klarman of Baupost, as he returned money to investors in the autumn of 2013, resonate eerily:

> *Investing today may well be harder than it has been at any time in our three decades of existence, not because markets are falling but because they are rising; not because governments have failed to act but because they chronically overreact; not because we lack acumen or analytical tools but because the underpinnings of our economy and financial system are so precarious that the unabating risks of collapse dwarf all other factors.*

CHINA

Since the rise of the West from around 1500, China has mostly been a weak peripheral presence often struggling just to maintain its borders. Distant, different and of relatively minor consequence to the evolving power centres of Europe, the historic Middle Kingdom featured little in the calculations of the emerging *great powers.*

More recently, the post-1945 inheritors of Western leadership in Washington – even with the surprising ascent of Mao – could also comfortably keep China at a significant distance from a centre stage dominated by global rivalry with the Soviet Union.

Unarguably, the rapid re-emergence of China is of historic import. The crucial catalyst has been its rapid economic development. On many measures, China has achieved an unprecedented leap forward. To cite just one statistic from Martin Wolf of the *Financial Times*: in 1990, 67% of the Chinese population lived below the World Bank definition of extreme poverty, but by 2014 this had fallen to just 1%.

In Wolf's apt words:

This progress is astounding.

While there are many reasons for this remarkable leap forward, the opportunity to pursue an effectively unlimited export-led growth policy has been critical. In the years since the collapse of Bretton Woods, the combined effect of fixing its currency to the US dollar, and preparing for and then joining the WTO, has exploded Chinese exports, economic growth and dollar reserves. Nixon cut money free, and Deng and his successors have ensured that China has increasingly hoovered it up.

As recently as 30 years ago, Sino-US trade was essentially irrelevant. Since then, the trade relationship has exploded, with the US consuming vastly more than the value of its output, and China doing the mirror opposite. By choosing to direct the vast bulk of its dollars into Treasury bonds, China is now the biggest private creditor of the US Federal Government.

Lord Mervyn King, the long-serving Governor of the Bank of England who retired in 2013, subsequently published an ambitious and wide-ranging book, *The End of Alchemy: Money, Banking & the Future of the Global Economy*. In the introduction, he credits his inspiration to put pen to paper to a senior Chinese central banker, and a conversation they had over dinner at the Diaoyutai State House in Beijing in the spring of 2011:

Bearing in mind the apocryphal answer of Premier Chou Enlai to the question of what significance one should attach to the French Revolution ("It was 'too soon to tell'"), I asked my Chinese colleague what importance he now attached to the Industrial

*Revolution in Britain in the second half of the 18th
century. He thought hard. Then he replied: "We in
China have learned a great deal from the West about
how competition and a market economy support
industrialisation and create higher living standards.
We want to emulate that". Then came the sting in the
tail, as he continued: "But I don't think you've quite
got the hang of money and banking yet".*

Little underlines the return of China to the top-table of
global influence as much as its successful navigation of
the global financial crisis.

In response to the crisis, China effected a dramatic
expansion of credit / debt *via* its banking and *shadow*
banking system. While this policy was broadly successful
in steering the economy through the crisis, many remain
concerned that it has left a fragile legacy worryingly
reminiscent of the pre-crisis West.

However, the conflation of the pre-and post-Lehman
experience of the developed world, and that of China
today, is mistaken.

As alluded to by Lord King's dinner companion in
Beijing, the Chinese financial system and its relationship
to the broader economy is fundamentally different by
design. More importantly, the differences suggest that
the worry of crisis will prove unfounded.

Notwithstanding the tentative steps towards capital
account liberalisation in recent years, the exposure of the
Chinese economy to foreign currency risk is non-existent.
Unlike its Asian counterparts in 1997, or the UK five

years before, China retains the power to settle its debts. Gross foreign currency external debt is a mere $800 billion – comfortably covered by the stock of foreign exchange reserves of $3.2 trillion. The Party / State thus retains ultimate control of how and when debt contracts are settled both domestically and internationally.

In practice, the key difference in the standard banking relationship between China and the West is that a single entity – the Party / State – is ultimately on both sides of the relationship. The Party / State is effectively both the borrower and the lender *via* its dominance of the non-bank economy, combined with its control of the banking system. In China, the opaque priorities of the Party / State, rather than the evolution of the credit cycle, always dominate.

China, of course, can direct its dollars wherever it chooses. While buying Treasury bonds has been the historic choice, future choices may well be different. Recently, for example, the enormously ambitious *Belt & Road initiative* has become a growing priority. Officially launched by President Xi in September 2013 as the *Silk Road Economic Belt*, and subsequently also known as the *One Belt, One Road initiative*, this stunningly ambitious project may yet overshadow the significance of the Marshall Plan.

At heart, the One Belt, One Road Road initiative is designed to boost trade and economic development across Asia and beyond, *via* an enormous infrastructure investment connecting China to countries around the globe. The potential scale is staggering: projects already planned or underway will impact 65% of the world's population, and are ultimately expected to account for the movement of 25% of all goods and services globally.

Sidelined for centuries, China is back. Able and clear-sighted leadership in Beijing has certainly played a role, but the stunning rise of China over recent decades has been effectively enabled by Washington. By cutting money free, the President who famously boasted that "Only a Nixon could go to China" opened the door not to a supplicant ally to help contain the Soviet Union, but to a resurgent rival of much greater, and likely enduring, strength.

EPILOGUE

In the years since the global financial crisis, the success of policymakers in piecing the Humpty Dumpty of the financial system back together has done little to change the risk at its heart. As summarised recently in the *Financial Times* by Martin Wolf:

> *Today, banks are less leveraged and better supervised than before the crisis. In the UK, retail banking is also ringfenced. Yet, the banks are leveraged at about 20 to 1: if the value of their assets falls by 5% or more, such a bank becomes insolvent.*

The compelling incentive to lend – to create money – also remains undiminished. Indeed, if anything it has increased. For example, as part of its current pitch to investors, top executives at Goldman Sachs are proudly trumpeting their aggressive expansion into lending. Having converted to a bank holding company in the teeth of the crisis, Goldman Sachs now enjoys full access to the emergency liquidity of the Fed, and its lending has surged to more than 10 times its 2012 level. More broadly, the explosive growth of the high yield bond and leveraged loan markets is striking.

Fundamentally, the global financial system remains the bewilderingly vulnerable structure bequeathed by Nixon: an unchanged combination of an unanchored global reserve currency, the Geithner doctrine, and privately-created endogenous money.

Growing more cognisant of this vulnerability in the years since the crisis, unsurprisingly the list of those suggesting alternatives has grown. Among others, the arguments of John Kay for *narrow banking*, Mervyn King for a *pawnbroker for all seasons*, Martin Wolf for *sovereign money*, and Adair Turner for *helicopter money* are all worthy of note. So too, the recent referendum on the *Vollgeld* initiative in Switzerland. Although soundly rejected on this occasion, the very fact that such a radically different monetary system was proposed in a country such as Switzerland shows that the likelihood of major change is undeniably increasing. The explosion of interest in cryptocurrencies is usefully seen in the same light.

Historically, the fracturing of trust, leadership and authority is often both a cause, and a symptom, of a fracturing monetary system. Having dispensed with many centuries of accumulated practice as recently as 1971, the current system is showing increasing signs of succumbing to the historical pattern. Worryingly, the words of the great George Bernard Shaw seem ever more relevant:

We learn from history that we learn nothing from history.

America First is looking more like *America Alone*. From climate change to trade and Iran to the broader Middle East, the US Administration seems determined to plough its own path.

The hegemony of the dollar and its unrivalled role as the global reserve currency has survived all challenges. Remarkably, even the break with gold, and the effective collapse of Bretton Woods in 1971, served only to strengthen – rather than weaken – its dominant position.

However, in stark contrast to his post-war predecessors, the current occupant of the White House has a radically different view of the power and responsibility of the US. The evidence is accumulating that the benign rationality of US engagement with the rest of the world is inverting.

The possibility that this may undermine the long-held position of the dollar at the heart of the global monetary system is now real and growing. A new era may be dawning where policymakers and investors across the globe are losing a long-standing constant, while the US faces the loss of a valuable privilege chasing a delusional fantasy to put *America First*.

The ghost of Nero seems to be stalking the White House.

In his insightful 2010 book, *Exorbitant Privilege: The Rise and Fall of the Dollar & The Future of the International Monetary System,* economic historian Barry Eichengreen concludes that the likelihood of continuing dollar dominance remains high. However, his conclusion comes with one significant, and possibly prescient, *caveat*:

Serious economic and financial mismanagement by the United States is the one thing that could precipitate flight from the dollar. And serious mismanagement is not something that can be ruled out. We may yet suffer a dollar crash, but only if we bring it upon ourselves.

SUGGESTED READING

Architects of Power: Roosevelt, Eisenhower & the American Century, Philip Terzian.

Banking: From Bagehot to Basel & Back Again, Mervyn King.

Between Debt & the Devil: Money, Credit & Fixing Global Finance, Adair Turner.

Can We Avoid Another Financial Crisis?, Steve Keen

Capitalism, Money, Morals & Markets, John Plender.

Coined: The Rich Life of Money and How Its History has Shaped Us, Kabir Sehgal.

Debt: The First 5,000 Years, David Graeber.

Debunking Economics: The Naked Emperor Dethroned?, Steve Keen.

Economic Possibilities for Our Grandchildren, John Maynard Keynes.

Europe: The Struggle for Supremacy, 1453 to the Present, Brendan Simms.

Exorbitant Privilege: The Rise & Fall of the Dollar & The Future of the International Monetary System, Barry Eichengreen.

Extreme Money: The Masters of the Universe & the Cult of Risk, Satyajit Das.

Fooled by Randomness: The Hidden Role of Chance in Life & in the Markets, Nassim Nicholas Taleb.

Franklin Delano Roosevelt: Champion of Freedom, Conrad Black.

Grand Pursuit: The Story of the People Who Made Modern Economics, Sylvia Nasar

Hall of Mirrors: The Great Depression, The Great Recession & the Uses – & Misuses – of History, Barry Eichengreen.

Instability in Financial Markets: Sources & Remedies, Steve Keen.

Keynes Hayek: The Clash that Defined Modern Economics, Nicholas Wapshott.

Keynes: The Twentieth Century's Most Influential Economist, Peter Clarke.

Money: The Unauthorized Biography, Felix Martin.

Money: Whence It Came, Where It Went, John Kenneth Galbraith

Other People's Money: Masters of the Universe or Servants of the People?, John Kay

Paper Promises: Money, Debt & the New World Order, Phillip Coggan.

Post-war: A History of Europe since 1945, Tony Judt.

Richard M. Nixon: A Life in Full, Conrad Black.

The Ascent of Money: A Financial History of the World, Niall Ferguson.

The Battle of Bretton Woods: John Maynard Keynes, Harry Dexter White.

The Colder War: How the Global Energy Trade Slipped from America's Grasp, Marin Katusa.

The Dog & the Frisbee, Andrew G Haldane.

The Economic Consequences of the Peace, John Maynard Keynes.

The End of Alchemy: Money, Banking & the Future of the Global Economy, Mervyn King.

The End of Influence: What Happens When Other Countries Have the Money, Stephen S. Cohen.

The Fall of Rome & the End of Civilization, Bryan Ward-Perkins.

The Federal Reserve & the Financial Crisis, Ben S. Bernanke.

The Federal Reserve: What Everyone Needs to Know, Stephen H. Axilrod.

The Global Minotaur: America, the True Origins of the Financial Crisis & the Future of the World Economy, Yanis Varoufakis.

The Great Crash 1929, John Kenneth Galbraith.

The Holy Grail of Macroeconomics: Lessons from Japan's Great Recession, Richard C. Koo.

The Keynes Solution: The Path to Global Economic Prosperity, Paul Davidson.

The Making of a New World Order, Benn Steil.

The Monopoly of Violence: Why Europeans Hate Going to War, James Sheehan.

The New Lombard Street: How the Fed Became the Dealer of Last Resort, Perry Mehrling.

The Origin of Financial Crises: Central Banks, Credit Bubbles & the Efficient Market Fallacy, George Cooper

The Party: The Secret World of China's Communist Rulers, Richard McGregor.

The Physics of Wall Street: A Brief History of Predicting the Unpredictable, James Owen Weatherall.

The Production of Money: How to Break the Power of Bankers, Ann Pettifor.

The Scramble for China: Foreign Devils in the Qing Empire, 1832-1914, Robert Bickers.

The Seven Deadly Innocent Frauds of Economic Policy, Warren Mosler.

The Shifts & Shocks: What We've Learned and Have Still to Learn from the Financial Crisis, Martin Wolf.

War & Gold: A Five-Hundred-Year History of Empires, Adventures & Debt, Kwasi Kwarteng.

Web of Debt: The Shocking Truth about Our Money System & How We Can Break Free, Ellen Hodgson Brown and Reed Simpson.

Where Does Money Come From? A Guide to the UK Monetary & Banking System, Josh Ryan-Collins, Tony Greenham, Richard Werner and Andrew Jackson.

Why Minsky Matters: An Introduction to the Work of a Maverick Economist, L. Randall Wray.

ABOUT THE AUTHOR

John joined KBI Global Investors in September 2014 and is a Senior Portfolio Manager on the global equity team. He has worked in Financial Markets since 1990 in roles spanning Fixed Income, Absolute Return and Equities. An economics graduate of UCD, he also holds post-graduate qualifications from TCD and DCU. He is a regular contributor of opinion pieces to the national press, and has had two collections published: *Troubled Times: Investing through the Troika Years* and *Sixty Shades of Sunday: Investment Thoughts*. The views expressed in this book are the author's own.

OAK TREE PRESS

Oak Tree Press develops and delivers information, advice and resources for entrepreneurs and managers. It is Ireland's leading business book publisher, with an unrivalled reputation for quality titles across business, management, HR, law, marketing and enterprise topics. NuBooks is its ebooks-only imprint, publishing short, focused ebooks for busy entrepreneurs and managers.

In addition, Oak Tree Press occupies a unique position in start-up and small business support in Ireland through its standard-setting titles, as well training courses, mentoring and advisory services.

Oak Tree Press is comfortable across a range of communication media – print, web and training, focusing always on the effective communication of business information.

OAK TREE PRESS

E: info@oaktreepress.com
W: www.oaktreepress.com / www.SuccessStore.com.